Cheame
Woocote
Saundersted
Chelsham
Tolworth court
Nonsuch
CROYDON
Chesington
Ewell
Woodmansturn
Ebsham court
Horton
Bansted
Chipsted
Ebsham
Katerham
Willmorepond
Burghhouse
Chaldon
COPTHORNE
Tadwort
Walton
Lymesfeild
OR EFFING
Mestham
Wilby
Hackstal
TANRID
Mychelham
Hedley
Gatton
HAM HUNDRED
RYGATE
Wiggy
Bletchingly
Godston
Buckland
RED
Nutfeild
Walkamsted
Colley
Reygate
Lingfeild stret
Pounchill
Lagham
Bechworth
HUND
Dorking
Reygate church
South parke
Woodhatch
Brokham
Flonesford
Douers
Ham
Bursto park
Craherst
Eywoode
HUNDRED
Lee
Sidlyn Hal
Kynnersly
Hourne
Newchapel
Lingfeild
Elmwoods borow
Shelwed
Bursto lodge
Smalfells
Bisli
Court
Leystret
Burstow
KINGE
Chappell
Temple
Norley
Hedge Court
Stipley bridg
Okeley
Newdigate
Whitgreene
Imberhorne
Crabber
HUNDREDE
Carlewood
Little parke
Rouant
Iffeldeou el
Worth
Iseylde
Ewhurst
Graue Ty
Rusper
Bennykeys
Crawley
Worth Forest
PART
Beaubuse
Tilgate
Warneham
Roffey
Shelley
Wakhurst
Horsham
Chesworth
Balcombe
Dersham
Handcroste
Ardingly
Sunfolde
Stamerbain
Seaint
Tyes
Itchingsold
Leonards
Slawgham
Sydney

(Joyce Hills.)

Ted Gomm.

15 Seltops Close.

Cranleigh.

Surrey. 276027

15 SELTOPS CLOSE
CRANLEIGH
SURREY
GU6 7JW
TEL (0483) 276027

Ted Gomm.

BYGONE CRANLEIGH

LIST OF ILLUSTRATIONS

The authors would like to thank the following, who allowed them to use their photographs: Cranleigh School, nos. 77, 78, 79, 80, 81, 82, 83; The Francis Frith Collection, nos. 12, 42, 50, 105, 106, 125, 129, 130; Guildford Muniment Room, nos. 13, 63; Guildford Museum, nos. 2, 110; The Rector, no. 14; The Surrey Archaeological Society, nos. 99, 102; Surrey County Library, nos. 17, 94; Les Field, 18, 19, 64.

ACKNOWLEDGEMENTS

Amongst the many organisations and individual members of the village who have helped us to produce this book, we would especially like to thank the following:

Mr. Leslie Field who gave so many hours of his time and patience in reproducing innumerable old and sometimes faded photographs that we entrusted to him, and we would also like to extend gratitude to Mrs. Field; Mrs. E. Dodsworth (née Corrin) who gave us permission to use her professional photographs and those of her father, the late Mr. Walter Corrin; Cranleigh History and Archaeology Society, who are the custodians of the Corrin pictures, for allowing us to borrow them; The Francis Frith Collection, which has given us permission to use some of their old postcards; Guildford Muniment Room; Guildford Museum; The Natural History Museum, South Kensington; and the Surrey Archaeological Society. Mr. I. B. Wyness very kindly allowed us to use his drawing of a locomotive, and the Cranleigh Bookshop checked lists of old postcard publishers. In the section on Cranleigh School, we would like to thank the Headmaster for giving us permission to publish pictures from the school's archives, Mr. Kenneth Hill for his memories and photography, and Mr. Alan Smith for his co-operation.

We are most grateful to the following who lent us their precious pictures: Mr. Don Nightingale, who was the first to advise, encourage and find us material, Mrs. W. Adams, Mrs. G. C. Brand, Mrs. J. Brown, Mr. Buckman, Mr. and Mrs. Budgen, Mr. T. R. Collins, Mr. T. Disley, Major D. Elliott, Mr. and Mrs. K. Fuller, Mrs. G. Gleed, Mrs. I. Howes, Mr. H. Jeacock, Mr. G. King, Mr. R. Noakes, Canon J. Roundhill (Rector), Mr. and Mrs. F. J. Shapland, Miss B. Stedman, Mr. and Mrs. H. Warrington, Mrs. E. Webb, Mr. and Mrs. W. Woodrow, Lens of Sutton, Cranleigh Fire Station, St John Ambulance Station, Cranleigh, The *Boy and Donkey*, and Cranleigh Camera Shop.

To those who gave us information, memories and guidance we would like to register our grateful appreciation: Mr. F. E. Cheeseman, Mr. P. C. Cheeseman, Mr. R. Foster, Mrs. E. Franklin, Mr. G. Harding, Mr. G. Howard, Mr. and Mrs. Sandford, Mr. P. C. Seymour and the Red Cross Training Centre, Barnet Hill, Wonersh, Surrey.

To those who recorded their reminiscences on tape we are especially indebted: the late Mr. C. Blogg (Headmaster of the old village junior school), the late Mrs. E. M. Budgen, sen., Mr. Bunce, the late Mr. Croxford (village cobbler), the late Mr. Henley (village policeman), Mr. and Mrs. H. Lade, the late Mr. Laker (whose tape was kindly given us by Mr. W. Loveridge), the late

Miss D. Morgan (verger of St Nicolas church), Mrs. K. Pirie, Mrs. P. C. Warrington, Mrs. W. Watson and Mrs. W. Whittington.

Finally, we would like to acknowledge the use we have made of material whose origin we have been unable to trace; and to anyone we have inadvertently omitted to thank, we sincerely apologise.

FOREWORD

Owing to the tremendous increase in Cranleigh's population over the past few years, we felt that newcomers as well as original villagers might be interested to learn about those who centuries ago shopped in the same street as themselves, attended the same church and worked in the fields now covered by modern housing estates. Through our written history and photographs we have tried to show Cranleigh throughout the ages, and the hard-won improvements made to drainage, road surfaces, the hospital, schools and the village hall.

Due to lack of space, our story only extends to the 1920s. There are still many gaps as we have only been able to use the material available but we hope that others will be stimulated to further research. To avoid any resemblance to a dry textbook, we have abbreviated the historical narrative as much as possible and supplied the captions under the photographs with personal memories as well as the necessary facts and dates, hoping that the result will entertain as well as inform.

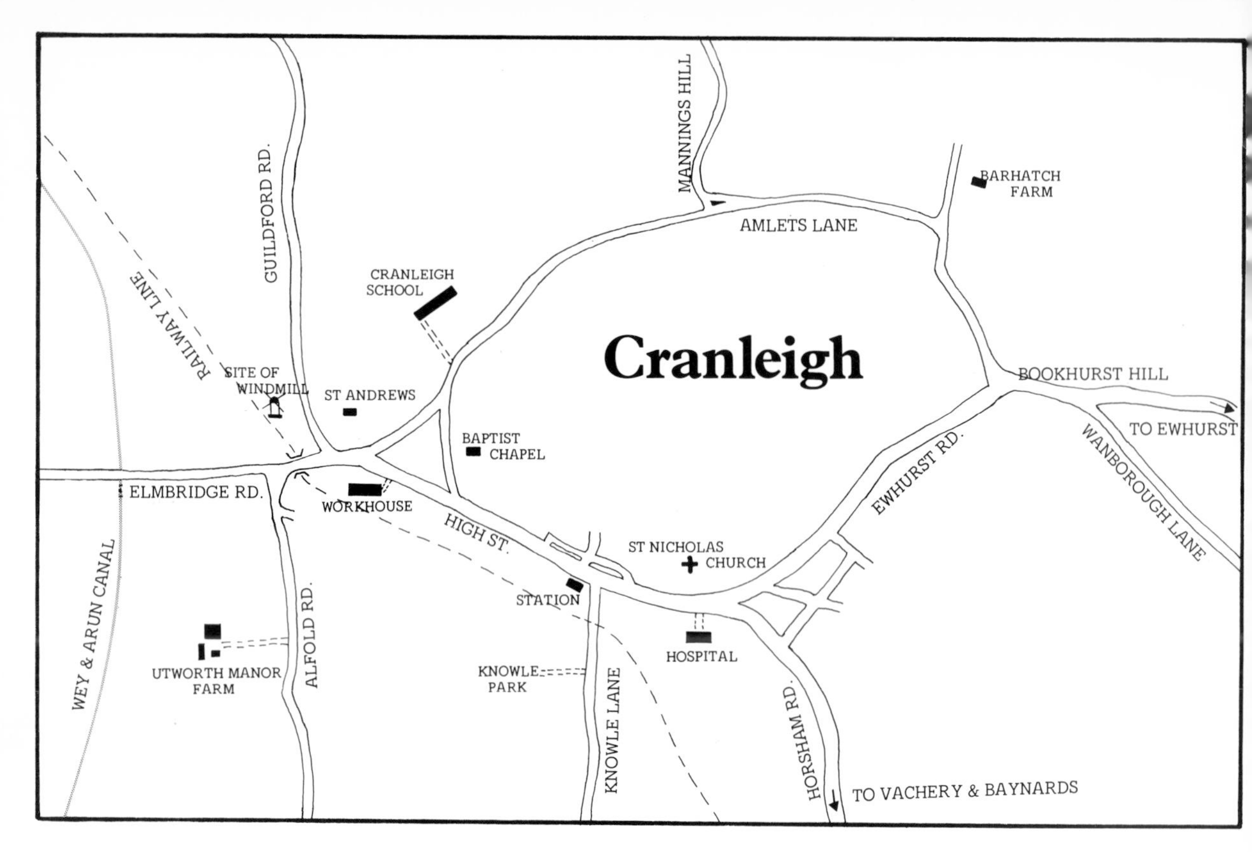

1. Map of Cranleigh covering the area mentioned in this book.

1a. A humorous postcard, *c.*1930.

INTRODUCTION

Cranleigh is situated in the Wealden valley, which was originally an estuary. The bones of iguanodons and other dinosaurs have been found near Smokejack's Brickyard, Ewhurst. Prehistoric fish swam in the estuary and their fossilised skeletons have been dug up both at Swallow Tiles in Cranleigh and Smokejack's. The dinosaur and fish bones from the two sites are in the Natural History Museum. Winkle beds, called Sussex marble, form strata in the clay, and Cranleigh cricket ground stands on a bed of this material.

The hills to the north of Cranleigh are composed of sandstone. The local water supply comes from springs lying on the blue gault clay at the bottom of these hills. In prehistoric times short grass, heather and pine trees grew on the hills, requiring little root depth and the valleys supported deciduous trees. Three thousand years of human occupation from Palaeolithic times left very little trace.

However, signs of Roman occupation have been found. A Romano-British villa at Rapsley, Cranleigh, was excavated in the 1930s and a Roman brickworks near Wykehurst was discovered in 1933-4. The nearest Roman road is believed to have climbed Jelly's Hollow to a temple on Farley Heath, which is thought to have been constructed before the first century A.D. This site must have been of considerable importance, as many artefacts have been found, including a hoard of gold coins found by a shepherd boy in 1848. The site of the temple was close to the road on Farley Heath, and is marked with stones.

About the beginning of the fifth century the last Roman legions withdrew. Fierce battles were fought in the hills around the area, and this district passed from one Saxon king to another. The late Mr. Harry Osgood of Ewhurst liked to claim that King Hardicanute gave the whole district to his ancestor, Thane Osgood.

The Old Manors of Cranleigh

In 1086 Cranleigh was part of the Blackheath Hundred. Queen Editha, wife of the Saxon king Edward the Confessor, held the district before the Norman Conquest. It was part of the vills of Shere, Gomshall and Bramley. It appears to have been known as Cranley before the days of recorded history and there have been several different spelling of the name. Its history seems to have been mainly connected with the manors of Vachery and Baynards. The hamlet of Vachery was the chief residence of the lords of the manors. Its name was originally 'Vaccaria', meaning a house to keep cows in, a dairy farm.

2. The remains of a Romano-British villa was discovered one-fifth of a mile from the Roman road at Rapsley, in the parish of Cranleigh. It was occupied from A.D. 80 until the end of the Roman occupation.

In 1086 Vachery belonged to the Earl of Surrey and in 1170 it was transferred to a Frenchman called Richard de Tonbridge. By this time the work force belonging to the estate had grown so large that it was decided to build a church for them. The nave of the parish church is believed to have been part of this original building. Vachery was mentioned in the grant of the manor of Shere by Roger de Tonbridge (Clere) to John Fitz-Geoffrey in 1244. Henry III gave deer to John to stock his park at Vachery and royal permission was granted for a weekly market and an annual fair in Cranleigh. In 1299 Vachery was given to Joan, wife of Theobald Le Boteler. She spent much of her time there and was a great benefactress of Cranleigh church. When she died in 1303, she was buried in the churchyard.

When Le Boteler's grandson, the Earl of Ormond, inherited the house, he brought Irish servants to work there. They quarrelled with some of the villagers and broke into the house of the local rector, James de Dalileye, smashing the furniture and setting fire to the building. The Ormond family were great patrons of the arts and learning, and encouraged the talents of their tenants, one of whom was named Thomas de Cranleigh, born at Wickhurst Farm at the bottom of Pitch Hill. With Ormond help, he became rector of Cranleigh in 1380, Lord Justice of Ireland, Chancellor of Oxford University and eventually Archbishop of Ireland.

3. Numerous craneries were once found on the shores of Vachery Lake, and from these Cranleigh (Craneley) derived its name. Royalty have hunted both herons and cranes in the district for centuries. In 1543 Lady Bray owned an iron forge at Vachery and water from the lake was used in the smelting process. It was later used as a reservoir by the Wey and Arun Canal Company.

John Audley became the next owner, followed by his son James. After he was beheaded on Tower Hill, James's estates were given to Sir Reginald Bray. The Brays continued to live at Vachery until the death of Sir Edward Bray in 1558, when it was abandoned and allowed to deteriorate. His son lived at Baynards and later sold Vachery. It was eventually purchased in 1605 by Sir Edward Onslow of Knoll and descended to other members of his family. By 1768 some of the estate had been split into parcels of land and farms, for example High Park and New Park.

The Baynards estate dates back to Saxon times when King Harold owned it. William the Conqueror gave this estate to his friend and comrade-in-arms, William Baynard, who gave his name to the property. Baynards was used as a hunting lodge and could be reached on horseback from Guildford Castle and Shere, where members of the court sometimes stayed. King William hunted there and complained of a half-cooked crane. In 1204 King John owned the estate and afterwards sold it for £1,000 to William de Braose, who later displeased the king. The estate was taken over by Robert Fitzwalter, who eventually led the barons against King John. Baynard House was described at this time as a 'castellated pile of heavy timbers of oak and wrought ragstone masonry, which stood like a cliff among a sea of magnificent oaks spreading in every direction for miles and miles around it, almost floating in a mighty sea of mud and swarming with wild hogs and wolves as well as robbers'.

In 1443 William Sydney, an ancestor of the Sidneys of Penshurst, came into possession of the estate. He was eventually buried in Cranleigh church. Baynards was next purchased by Sir Reginald Bray who added more land to the estate. He arranged the marriage of Elizabeth, daughter of Edward IV, to Henry VII, which marked the end of the Wars of the Roses. Baynards passed down through the Bray family until it was sold to George More of Losely, who rebuilt the mansion and took up residence. He was a relation of Sir Thomas More (Henry VIII's Lord Chancellor) who was executed at the king's command. His head was hung on London Bridge, but later smuggled to Baynards by his daughter, Margaret Roper, where it was kept in a painted charter chest. It was finally buried with her when she died. Margaret's daughter, Elizabeth, was the second of the four wives of Sir Edward Bray.

A flintlock pistol, a tournament shield carried on the Field of the Cloth of Gold, a breastplate and helmet, all belonging to Henry VIII, were among the treasures once housed in the old mansion.

4. Oliver Cromwell stayed at Knowle and his staff were billeted at Oliver House. In return for Cranleigh's hospitality, Cromwell bestowed on the village a charter granting the right to hold two fairs each year. The parchment charter was kept at Knowle for many years and a facsimile now hangs in Cranleigh School library.

The estate passed through the hands of a few other owners before it was purchased by Richard, 1st Lord Onslow, who lived at Knowle, Cranleigh. However, he later moved to Clandon Park so as to be nearer to London and after he died in 1717 the house and grounds became neglected. They remained so until restored by the Bishop of Durham's son, the Rev. C. H. Townsend. By the mid-18th century the property belonged to the Thurlow family who made further restorations.

There were five other manors in the district:

Shoxhall: old spelling of Snocks Hill. This is thought to have been part of the manor of Pollingfold in Ewhurst.

Holdhurst: in Edward III's reign this was the property of Thomas Holdhurst whose family held it for many years. Later it belonged to the Onslow family.

Utworth Manor: (old spelling Otteworth or Utworth, meaning 'the outer farm'. It extended to the parish of Wonersh and in the reigns of Henry VI and Edward IV it became the property of Walter de Otteworth. It was later also owned by the Onslow fmaily.

Redinghurst: once held by the manor of Utworth and released to Sir John Reddinghurst for 5s per annum.

Knowle: (old spelling Knoll or Knole). Built by Robert of Knoll around 1303. Towards the end of the 15th century it was conveyed to Robert Harding, who was a goldsmith and alderman of London. It descended through his family until it passed into the hands of the Onslow family. The Onslow family was important in the village during the 16th and 17th centuries. During this period they gradually acquired the ownership of many of the manors of the district. Richard Onslow succeeded to Knowle in 1616 and settled there after his marriage. During the Civil War, Oliver Cromwell once stayed with him. However, Richard appears to have had an interest in both sides, defending Cromwell and also sending money to the king.

Industries and Communications

During the 13th century, glass workers came over from France and began a glassmaking business. Kilns were established at Sydney Wood, Alfold, Chiddingfold and at Sumersbury Farm near Ewhurst. The industry flourished and supplied clear and coloured glass for the windows of Westminster Abbey. An example of this work was once to be found in the parish church, showing a genealogical tree indicating the descent of Christ from King David. In 1820, the window was kicked to pieces by the boys from one of the dame schools. This industry gradually declined during the late 16th century, and Jean Carre, one of the last skilled workers, died in 1572 and was buried in Alfold churchyard.

During the 15th and 16th centuries iron foundries began to spring up. Forges were kept busy casting cannon and cannon balls. Gunpowder mills were set up in Chilworth. Lady Bray owned a forge at Vachery and John Lambert owned one in Cranleigh. Yet another one was worked by Robert Woodheie and there were probably even more in the village.

The development of the industry altered the countryside. Woods were cut down to feed furnaces, and rich landowners also cut down their oaks for ironmaking and shipbuilding, while commoners were not allowed to cut wood even for fires and cooking. After the defeat of the Armada in 1588 an Act was passed prohibiting the felling of trees for use in the ironmaking industry which were more than one foot square at the stub and were within 14 miles of a navigable river. The inadequate roads, which were little more than rough, muddy tracks, flooded and often impassable in winter, made things very difficult for the iron industry. The heavy waggons destroyed any road surface that existed, and owners were obliged to carry, with every load of iron, a load of gravel, stone or similar material to repair the damage. The industry proved to be uneconomical and gradually declined.

In the 18th century 'turnpike trusts' were instituted, private companies which contracted to keep the roads in repair and in return were allowed to levy tolls on traffic. A turnpike trust was set up to improve the road from London to Brighton. When it was completed in 1794, the 55-mile journey was cut from two days to five and a half hours. The new turnpike road branched off from another one leading from Loxwood to Guildford. It then passed through Run Common, Cranleigh Street (now called High Street), Ellens Green, through Broadbridge Heath and on to Horsham. James Child and John Putock are just two of the local folk who helped build the road. The names of many other village labourers on the turnpike are recorded. At a later date labourers were supplied from Cranleigh Workhouse to break stones and keep the roads in repair.

5. Barhatch Farmhouse was said to have been a favourite rendezvous during the 18th and 19th centuries, when smugglers passed through Cranleigh on the route from Shoreham, on the coast, to London. The remains of a pit used for cockfighting has recently been found in the garden. The track to the north and south of Cranleigh is still known as Smugglers' Lane.

6. The canal linking the rivers Wey and Arun was officially opened on 29 September 1816. The Earl of Egremont who was Chairman of the Company, friends, shareholders and official dignitaries, celebrated the occasion on board four decorated barges at Alfold. Accompanied by the music of two bands and loud cheers, they set off for Guildford via Cranleigh.

There were five toll gates in the area, situated at Cranleigh Common, Leathern Bottle, Gaston Gate, Ellens Green and Alfold Crossways. The local inhabitants were dismayed, as they could ill afford the charges imposed upon them, the average wage being approximately 12d (1s), per week. The price for 65 cows to go through the gates was 17d, for two-horse teams 20d, and one cart cost 6d. In addition, people were fined if carts, etc., exceeded the recommended weight or size, and if animals were found straying near the road they were impounded. To recover them the owner had to pay 5s, plus costs, or within five days they would be sold.

At the beginning of the 19th century it was felt that there was a great need for a short, easy route between the ports of London and Arundel. Plans were made to build a new waterway, linking the Wey and the Arun to save the long journey around the Kent coast. To achieve this, the Wey and Arun Junction Company was formed in 1813. Lord Egremont, who owned a considerable amount of land in Sussex, became chairman of the company, providing much of the money and initiative. When the canal was completed in 1816, it linked the Wey at Shalford to the Arun at New Bridge, passing through Bramley, Run Common and Loxwood. The construction gave work to many local craftsmen, as well as to Irishmen and French prisoners from the Napoleonic Wars.

Rules were drawn up governing the use of the canal. Boats were to be built in a certain fashion and the name of boat owners and the weight of the boats were to be painted on the outside. Tolls were paid on all goods and passengers transported. Owners were answerable for damage done by their boats, horses and servants. Fishing rights were reserved for the lords of the manors, where the canal ran through their lands. A penalty was imposed on bargemen carrying guns and nets to take or destroy fish or game.

Trade and industry were improved by this new and easy way to transport goods. Coal was then able to travel from South Wales to Arundel by lighters. Slow-moving sail barges then carried it to Cranleigh, unloading at Elmbridge Wharf. Other boats transported general merchandise, including groceries, wheat, walking sticks, etc. The goods were unloaded and taken by waggon to their destinations – not always easy as the roads were still appalling. The charcoal business on Run Common, owned by Richard Medland, was able to take full advantage of the improved transport facilities, the canal and the wharf on Run Common.

The lake in the grounds of Vachery House was used as a reservoir for the canal but was not able to supply enough water and the barges could not be fully laden. Two windmill pumps were built to remedy the situation, Cranleigh Mill in 1833 and Birtley Mill in 1834. Around the early 1840s George Snelling lived in a cottage close to the windmill. He worked for the canal company and one of his jobs was to minimize the leakage of water through the lock gates by throwing in sawdust.

When the Horsham to Guildford Railway was opened in 1865, it took much of the trade away from the canal. The canal boats made slow progress, having to rely on horses to pull them, and there were delays as the locks were emptied out. The canal closed because the traffic was greatly diminished and no longer yielded a profit to the shareholders. It was sold by auction in 1870.

The line had five stations, Bramley, Cranleigh, Baynards, Rudgwick and Slinfold; there was also to be a junction at Christ's Hospital. There were great celebrations when the line was opened. The train was decorated, bands played and everyone was given a free ride. Only the Rudgwick people were left out and they were furious. This was because the Board of Trade inspector refused permission for the engine to stop at Rudgwick until gradient alterations were made.

After the railway was built, the effects of the Industrial Revolution began to be felt. Postal services were brought up to date as the mail was carried on the train. Public water and gas supplies were brought to the village. The drainage ditch at the side of The Street was filled in and a new system built. Local councils were set up and they took over many of the responsiblities of the parish council. Cranleigh's first police station was built. The village street became known as the High Street, and the old spelling of the name 'Cranley' changed to the modern spelling 'Cranleigh'.

Daily Life in the Village

In the Middle Ages the lord of the manor was at the top of the system and serfs and villeins at the bottom. The latter belonged to their lord and worked mostly on the land; their payment was in food and shelter. They were obliged to ask permission to marry, were unable to leave the estate and when the manor changed hands were passed on to the next lord. Over the centuries this

7. The local doctor, Doctor Ellery provided this obelisk to commemorate the opening of the turnpike road which passed through Cranleigh. When King George IV travelled to his Brighton Pavilion, he found the deeply-rutted roads extremely uncomfortable. Tolls were imposed to provide money for improvements. This made travelling easier but more expensive for the local villagers.

Smithbrook
TURNPIKE.
Monday
2 June 1760
One Shilling.

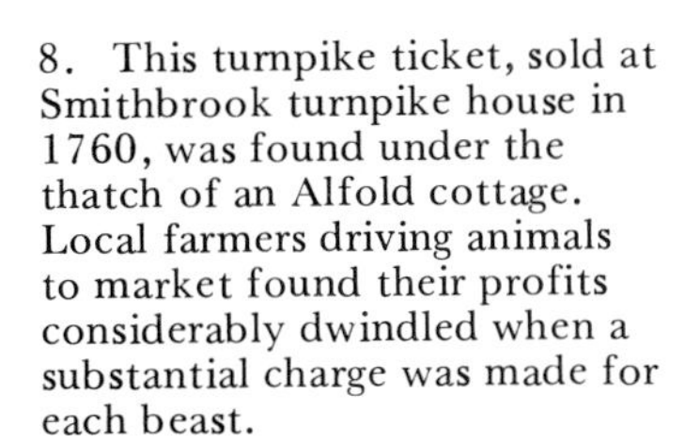

8. This turnpike ticket, sold at Smithbrook turnpike house in 1760, was found under the thatch of an Alfold cottage. Local farmers driving animals to market found their profits considerably dwindled when a substantial charge was made for each beast.

changed. The lord of the manor no longer owned his workers but was still the head of the community. Next in order of importance came the rector, followed by the large landowners and then the farmers, who were usually tenants. The actual work was done by the labouring classes, who owned no land and usually lived in a cottage owned by their employers. They lived from hand to mouth, eking out a living by exploiting the resources of the uncultivated waste lands.

Village life revolved round the church and the rector. Vestry meetings were held to deal with parish matters. These covered a wide range of subjects – public worship, discipline, care of the poor and infirm and the beating of the bounds to establish parish boundaries. The earliest church register to survive dates back to 1566.

The following cases were obtained from the Poor Rate Books and give some idea of life in the past:

1663: Emery Wilson, Albury, husbandman fined £20 to keep the peace towards William Tickner, a Cranleigh husbandman.
1665: Francis Farley and George Dunstable, yeoman, late of Cranleigh, have on several occasions been common poachers, taking hares and pheasants with traps.
1661: William Hamshene of Cranleigh, 16 years yeoman, did not attend church for three months.
1871: Guildford Bench gave six strips of birch rod to a boy of eight for stealing an inkstand and memo book worth 4s 3d.

The parish constable was responsible for law and order in the parish. However, it seemed that in Cranleigh extra help was needed, for in 1791 a friendly society was formed. The purpose of this society was to give protection against lawbreakers. Some old Cranleigh names mentioned were Chennell, Tickner, Ryde and Butler.

In the 19th century a fund of £75 was set up so that the churchwardens and overseers could assist people to emigrate: in 1843 four young men were given assistance to emigrate to New Zealand. Leslie Elliott with his wife and seven children decided to try their luck in America. They were assisted with their passage and given two sovereigns each. After landing, their expenses to their destination were paid and each family given another sovereign.

In 1723 an Act of Parliament allowed parishes to build their own workhouses and refuse relief to those who would not enter them. In 1794 a large grey workhouse was built on Cranleigh Common. It stood in 11 acres of grounds and was situated behind Parkgate Cottages. It was designed to contain 150 inhabitants, but only about 20 lived there at any one time. Adjoining the main building was a pest house where infectious cases of illness were isolated. The building also contained a room to die in. On arrival at the workhouse, husbands and wives under the age of 60 were parted and obliged to live in opposite wings of the house. Their personal clothes were taken and grey workhouse worsted given in exchange. A usual three-month order to the Cranleigh workhouse would include a stout calico, dyed frocking, fustian grey cloth, Manchester tape, used before elastic was invented, and worsted stockings.

Outings were limited to two per week – namely two church services – unless special permission was given. The workhouse inmates were segregated from the rest of the congregation when attending church. Able-bodied inmates were expected to work; the men breaking stone to mend parish roads, or grave-digging. The women did various forms of housework, sewing and laundry. Both sexes made and sold shoes and sorted out old bones. Soup dinners were provided on Mondays and pork on Thursdays. For misbehaviour, plain bread was substituted for meat.

Regular meetings of the Workhouse Board of Governors used to take place at the *Onslow Arms*. At a typical session, they decided to put a stop to the customary gifts of food from local shops, and to cut the children's allowance. They agreed to forcibly evict an old couple named Mr. and Mrs. Charles Potterton from their cottage and send them to the workhouse. A Mr. and Mrs. Henry Jarret were ordered by the Governors to the workhouse. Newcomers had to arrive before

8.30 a.m.: if they were late, a fine of 5s was levied on each man and woman. A young girl from the workhouse, named Leah Edwards, was sent to be a housemaid to a Mr. G. Saddler, and was to be paid 1s a week, food and clothes provided except shoes and bonnet.

The building proved too costly to support and in 1821 the west wing was pulled down. At the same time the dying room and the hospital wing were converted into tenements for homeless families, each one to contain six people, and six almshouses and a cottage were made available for the homeless. In 1842 the workhouse was sold for £415 to Lord Grantly. In 1847, when it was being used to store corn, it caught fire and a large part of it was destroyed. The remains of the workhouse were renovated and lived in by Cooper Sutherland, a farmer, until the end of the First World War.

Another duty of the Church was beating the bounds (perambulating), a custom which dates back to Anglo-Saxon times and which continued until it was possible to make accurate maps. The boundaries of Cranleigh were walked over regularly and the last records of the perambulations were in 1847. On these days the parishioners were allowed to trespass on private land or pass through private houses when necessary. Sometimes there were small disputes with Shere concerning the boundaries, which is not surprising as some of the markings were simply recorded as 'Holly tree marked C and S to the left of the pond' or 'A crooked fir tree'. To ensure that the village boys would remember the exact position of the bounds, they were 'bumped', that is, swung against a hard object such a tree which was close to the boundary. William Elliot, aged 13 years, is recorded as one of the boys who was bumped.

Cranleigh was well provided with 'dame schools'. There were at least five in the village in 1846. As less than half the population could read and write anyone able to impart even a smattering of these accomplishments could form a small private school and charge a fee. However, children of working-class families were expected to contribute to the family income as soon as possible and had little or no education. In 1847 a National School for the poor was opened. Archdeacon Sapte gave the site and an appeal was made for finance, but less than half the amount needed was raised. The Rev. Thomas Thurlow of Baynards came to the rescue and gave the rest of the money. The lord of the manor supplied the stone for the building, which was quarried from Pitch Hill and brought down to the village in the local farmers' carts. It was a somewhat low building with only two classrooms. In rather cramped quarters at the back of the school lived the headmaster, Mr. Poor, and his wife. Cranleigh School, founded in 1863, was originally a county boarding school, particularly for farmers' sons. When the school opened there were 22 boarders and four day boys. The school thrived and the number of boys increased rapidly. It was incorporated as a public school by royal charter in 1898.

For many centuries, there was no form of organised medical aid. Country folk managed as best they could, treating illness with herbs and potions made by themselves. The services of a 'wise woman' were often called in. In 1812 Dr. John Ellery was the resident medical worker, and also acted as midwife. He was later joined by Dr. Napper. In these early days leeches were used for blood letting and until 1900 doctors were expected to supply their own dressings. The rector, Archdeacon Sapte, and Dr. Napper realised the inadequacies of the medical facilities and in 1859 founded the village hospital, the first of its kind in the country. Its main purpose was to relieve the suffering of the poor and needy. However, higher classes also benefited from it. It was maintained by the generosity of local subscribers who gave money and gifts. An old cottage, once the vicarage, was fitted out with wards, an operating room and a nurse's bedroom. This period also saw the beginning of district nursing, so that patients could be treated at home, although the bad roads and lack of suitable transport made the nurses' job doubly difficult.

There were several large estates and scattered farms in the area, but much of the countryside was still wild and unpopulated in the mid-19th century. There were two farms in 'The Street' (as it was called at that time), Ivy Hall and Stone Wall farms, and there were several others in the vicinity. The windmill was on the common, where the cattle grazed and poultry roamed. James Peter's house and forge were a short distance away, near the village centre. Almost opposite, was the toll gate cottage, in which lived Master Hersey, who was in charge of collecting the tolls.

Many of the villagers worked on the estates and farms. Most of the craftsmen did work related to agriculture, as blacksmiths, wheelwrights, millers and the like.

There were a few shops along the village street to meet the needs of the villagers. Running along the south side of The Street was a drainage ditch. To reach the shops and buildings on this side, small wooden bridges had to be crossed. The village stocks stood near the almshouses until 1840. When they were removed a vestry meeting was held 'To consult as to the priority of building a cage for the confinement of disorderly persons'.

In 1846 a mail cart came daily from Guildford. Previously the mail had been brought from the same town every day in a van drawn by two mastiffs who had to carry stout Master Sylvester as well as the bag. This mode of transport had taken the place of the walking mail man who used to bring the letters twice a week in two rush baskets.

During the 18th and 19th centuries the area was the haunt of smugglers. Luxury goods such as tea, tobacco and spirits were shipped illegally into the country. Cranleigh was on the route of some of these runs. The gangs landed at Shoreham in Sussex at high tide, loaded their goods on to pack mules, then rode to Hurtwood in Cranleigh the same night. Their route took them up Jelly's Hollow and Horseblock Hollow. The smugglers travelled at night, keeping to the quieter paths and lanes. One or two of them would steal out at night to the villages, selling their goods to the public house keepers, squires and village folk. Most of the villagers turned a blind eye to these activities and in return benefited from them. The tombs in Cranleigh churchyard were one of the many places used to conceal the contraband. The *Old Windmill Inn*, Ewhurst, which is believed to contain a false roof, and the nearby windmill, were two of their haunts.

The Plates

9. (*opposite, above*) Edwardian skating scene on Vachery Lake.

10. (*opposite, below*) This picture of St Nicholas's church was taken in about 1840. After the malthouse and cottage had been pulled down in 1867, their position was marked by four wooden posts. The present path in the churchyard passes over the site. The area occupied by the brick wall and cottages now forms part of the graveyard. The south porch was added in 1863.

11. (*above*) The east window of the parish church (photographed in the latter half of the last century) shows the original stained glass which, together with ten other windows, was shattered by a flying bomb in 1944. They have all been replaced with leaded windows of plain glass which has the effect of making the interior of our old church unusually light.

12. (*right*) In 1880 the churchyard was enlarged as far as the main road. The lychgate was designed by Woodyer, the Surrey architect, as a memorial to John Bradshaw of Knowle. Woodyer also designed the church porch in memory of Dr. Ellery, the present rectory (built 1864), and the drinking fountain on the cricket ground. This photograph was taken in 1908.

13. St Nicholas's was first built by the Norman owners of Vachery (a large estate and dairy farm) in 1170 for their workers on what was thought to be an old Saxon site. It probably only originally covered the area of the present nave. The church was enlarged at the end of the 12th century. This photograph shows the churchyard before its extension to the main road.

14. There has been a rectory on thi site since at least 1296 when James de Dalileye was Rector. Irish servant from Vachery broke into the buildin and burnt it to the ground, after which it was rebuilt. The remains of a medieval moat can still be seen. This building was standing before 1863.

15. John Henry Sapte was Archdeacon of Surrey, and a Canon of Winchester. He was born in December 1821. In 1846 he was nominated as rector of Cranleigh and held the position for 60 years. One of the founders of the National School and the village hospital, he died at the age of 84.

16. Building the Methodist church in 1904: back, Tom Craft, Alan Kelsey, Bert Lasham, Jim Killick, Ted Lasham: front, ? George Tickner, Fred Tanner, ?, J. Page, Ted Dubbins.

17. This Baptist chapel was built in 1889, under the pastorage of Mr C. B. Barringer. Mr and Mrs George Holden and Mr Barringer started a day school for 32 children in a room at the side of the chapel. The school was closed in 1884.

18. View of the Common, 80 years on, standing by the same pond as the small boy in the previous picture. The photograph shows the rare variety of maple trees called *acer schwedern,* now grown to their full size. Their size and deep red colouring in autumn give villagers and visitors great pleasure every year.

19. The Baptist chapel and the adjoining burial ground was opened in 1828. The pastor was John Holden. The chapel grounds are subject to a two thousand-year lease, which commenced in 1603. The payment for this lease is one red rose per year. Prior to this, Pear-tree Cottage on the Common was used for Baptist services.

20. A view of the church and Lucks Green from the Horsham Road, photographed in 1906. The police station now stands behind the rustic bridge on the right of the picture. The rector's cow-stalls once stood here.

21. In 1846 there were four or five dame schools in the village. Parents paid a few pence a week for their child to learn the three Rs but many villagers with large families found even these fees beyond their reach.Once the National School was available the dame schools gradually disappeared. This particular cottage in the High Street has long since been pulled down.

22. On Empire Day, all English schoolchildren paraded to honour the monarch and flag, and enjoyed a half-holiday. In the background can be seen the church tower and the Lady Peak Institute.

23. This photograph was taken in about 1850 before the hall was added to the school (built 1847). The tower of the church was not yet shaded by the great cedar of Lebanon planted by Archdeacon Sapte after his honeymoon. The two white houses have now been demolished.

24. The old National School was finally closed in 1964. The premises were then used for some years by the church youth group for table tennis. Later they lay empty and vandalised until the Art Society, Cranleigh Players and Camera Club took over the building to form the present Cranleigh Arts Centre Limited.

25. (*above*) The *Boy and Donkey* was for many years the scene of the re-enactment of Civil War conflicts.

26. (*left*) Once the most conspicuous mill in Surrey, the Ewhurst or Upper mill, which stands 800 feet above sea level, is now almost obscured by trees. A former mill mentioned in 1648 belonged to Richard Evelyn's wife. The present mill, built in 1845, was last working in 1885. It was blown down in a gale when the wind suddenly changed. The miller, though still inside, escaped injury. It is now a private dwelling.

'7 (*right*) The windmill on the Common was overed in weather boarding and rested on ricks. The four sails were shuttered, working n the principle of venetian blinds. They were et so near the ground that dogs were sometimes truck by them. When one of the sails broke in 882, a gas engine was installed. Wellers, the orn merchants, bought the mill the same ear and erected the outbuildings.

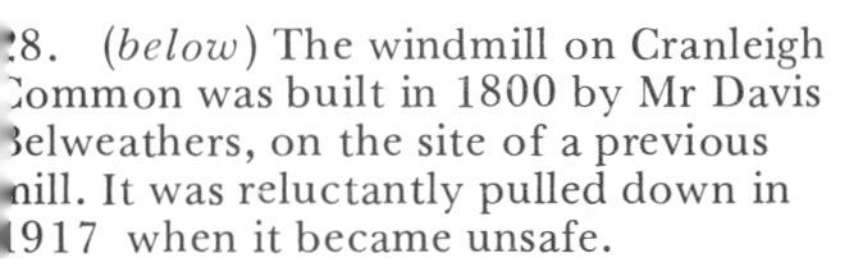

:8. (*below*) The windmill on Cranleigh Common was built in 1800 by Mr Davis Belweathers, on the site of a previous nill. It was reluctantly pulled down in 1917 when it became unsafe.

29. (*right*) Cheesman's paint shop is in the foreground, and the wheelwright's shop is in the background. James Cheesman started the firm and after his death his mother Esther continued the business. The building was situated close to the National School and has since been pulled down.

30. (*left*) This picture shows the workmen of Cheesman & Sons in 1923. Two metal rails called 'skids' were hung down from the top room and carts were guided up through the doorway to be painted in a dust-free atmosphere by Jim Laker. Doors remained firmly shut until the paint was dry. On the far right is Christopher Cheesman, and next to him in his leather apron is Heber Cheesman.

31. Bruford Brewery Stables were pulled down in 1913. The Old Court House is now built on the site. A great pile of brewery bottles was found behind the stables when they were demolished.

32. This photograph shows Bruford's brewery where spirits and mineral waters were manufactured, and was taken in the early 1900s. It was situated next to the *Three Horseshoes* public house; its site is now occupied by the Cranleigh Motors Garage. An old villager recalls 'the smell of hops and potatoes . . . and the rattle of the wooden clogs worn by the men working in the brewery'. The village stocks once stood in front of the *Three Horseshoes*; but they were taken down in 1840.

33. A group of workers from Bruford's brewery.

34. Outside Holden's yard, showing some of the vehicles that were later burnt in the fire. All the trees have now disappeared and the house itself has been demolished to make room for a supermarket.

35. Holden's sawmill and timberyard occupied an acre of ground behind the present-day Budgeon's supermarket. They employed 120 men and were well known for high quality work. The man in the top-hat is Mr Ebenezer Holden, the owner. The mills were famous for the manufacture of bell frames made from local oak, some exported as far as Australia and Russia.

36. In 1906 a fire broke out in Holden's timberyard early one Friday morning in June. Damage amounted to £10,000 destroying the men's personal tools and throwing them out of work. The firm was uninsured. The fire engine from Guildford was summoned by the landlord of the *Greyhound* (which stood on the site of our modern post office) who cycled to Guildford for their assistance.

37. Warren's, the builders, succeeded Holden's after the great fire. Some of their men are seen here standing outside Stroud House. Those who have been identified are Mr. Witchen, Harry Lee, Ted Budgen, Jim Sawnford and Bill Foster.

38. The gentleman in the bowler hat is Mr. Warren, the builder. Mr. and Mrs. Thorpe are in the middle of the picture and Mr. Hillman Attwell is between them. They are attending the opening ceremony of one of the new roads.

SAMUEL B. HASE
M. INST. M. & CTY
ENGINEER & SURVEY

9. (*opposite, above*) In the confusion and xcitement, the lorry pulling the fire-engine vertumed. After the destruction caused by ie fire Warren's moved to Holden's old yard ırther down the High Street.

0. (*opposite, below*) James Manfield, who wned Hollyhock Brickworks in 1903. astonia keep their coaches on this site, hich is now an industrial estate.

1. (*above*) Photographed in 1886, when the Collins family owned the premises now called 'Home & Gardens'. Mr. obert Collins was killed in the First World War, and his brother decided to sell the grocery and bakery shop and t up on his own next door as a pork butcher. Collins sausages are now so popular that they are sold to visitors from ll over the world.

2. (*below*) By the early 1900s the tree had been removed, gas lamps, and even telegraph poles installed along ie village street. The gateway led to sheds at the rear of the shop where the pigs were killed and the pork cured.

43. The staff of Collins's shop, about 1912: left to right in black suits, Robert Collins and George Collins; in white coat, centre, Harry Moyer; on his immediate right, Bill Annells. A few old villagers can still remember old Mrs. Collins 'looking like Queen Victoria sitting just inside the door dealing with the cash, and she never made mistakes!'.

44. At the beginning of the century, Hibbs' Bakery was a coal merchant owned by Mr Windsor. Just before the First World War, Mr Germany turned the premises into a bakery, which was later bought by Mr Tom Cornwall, who had previously been the landlord of the *Greyhound*, now the post office.

45. This shows David Mann's shop decorated for Queen Victoria's Diamond Jubilee in 1897. There were once three shops in these premises; one was an iron foundry owned by Mr. Champion. Some of the fire baskets he made can still be found locally. During alterations a hidden room was discovered; inside was a very old printed copy of the Ten Commandments.

46. In the days before the cottage became Mann's shop, the village doctor lived in the 'ironmongery' side. He apparently disapproved of his two sons because he 'cut them off with a shilling' in his will. This picture was taken in the early 1900s when Cromwell Cottage was still a separate building.

47. A contingent of Mann's vehicles lined up outside the *Onslow Arms* public house. During the First World War, Mann's supplied the Government with great quantities of charcoal for the manufacture of gunpowder. At the beginning of the century there used to be a fruit stall on the grass outside the *Onslow Arms* every weekend.

48. Walker's the newsagents, a 16th-century cottage, is now a gentleman's outfitter. Hight's the greengrocer, a 17th-century building, has become a photographic shop. Both buildings are roofed with Horsham slabs. The *Onslow Arms* is still a public house. The alley between the two cottages is known as Harley Street.

49. The gas lamp stands outside Tyler's shop, once Ivy Hall Farm. To the left of the motor cycle and side car now stands the village bus shelter where the village brass and wind band used to play every Saturday evening.

50. This picture was taken in about 1890. Weller's auctioneers later became the London & County Bank. The bank was next door before it moved to its larger premises shown in No. 51. Further on still is Parsons' the saddler.

51. The London & County Bank, standing in the middle of this picture, was badly flooded in 1903. This photograph was taken two years later. The lower half of this bank is now Cosco's electrical shop.

52. This shop, then Blanch the butcher's, was later bought by Mr. Nightingale who turned it into a furniture and china store. Years ago the passage between the butcher and Mr. Henry Rowland's house next door led to a post office run by Mr. Crewdson, cabinet maker and postmaster. Nightingale's was pulled down to make room for extensions to the hospital.

53. London House was a draper's shop, owned by a Mr. Briggs and his three sons. It was later enlarged and bought by Gammons, a larger firm of drapers. On the death of Gammons' owner, the premises were sold and pulled down. A bank and wine shop now stand on the site.

54. Gammons' shop can be seen immediately in front of the watch-clock sign board. It was a very popular drapery. The clock and jewellery shop was once the home of the only dentist in Cranleigh. Before his arrival in the village, patients went to the doctor who gave them 1s for a tot of whisky to kill the pain before extracting the tooth.

55. Over the last 150 years the post office has been housed in various Cranleigh buildings. This picture shows it at the High Street end of Knowle Lane. It was finally moved to its modern site next door to Collins' shop.

56. The Old Bank House, which was the first bank in Cranleigh, was later turned into a coal office for many years. However, when the railway station was closed, both the coal office and W. H. Smith & Sons next door, were dismantled to make way for the new shopping precinct. During the demolition, an old penny was found next to the bank's foundation stone.

57. These two shops, once an orchard and now a funeral parlour and a shoeshop stand on the opposite side of the road to the old Toll House (now pulled down). It is recorded that in 1847 a Master Hersey collected the tolls. In about the 1890s the house was converted into a sweet shop.

58. This shows the Horseshoe Lane entrance to Brain's butcher's shop and slaughter house. Carts were washed in the pond. The house has long since been converted into a private dwelling.

59. Brown's Pond, Horseshoe Lane. The house on the left, called Wakehurst, was once a coal merchant's. He delivered the coal by horse and cart. The two horses were said to be outstandingly beautiful. Later it became the headquarters for the Gastonia Coach Company, started by George Weller from Gaston Gate—hence the name.

60. A modern picture of Brown's Pond. To the left can be seen part of Pear Tree Cottage where early Baptist meetings were held.

61. The corner shop on Ewhurst Road was Mrs. Nightingale's sweet shop, now converted into a petfood store. The cottages are still standing.

62. Traction engines are rarely seen today. They were widely used in the early part of this century for haulage. This one, owned by David Mann, is standing on the ground now occupied by Rowland House.

63. (*opposite, above*) Cranleigh High Street, looking west at the turn of the century. There were very few signposts in those days and old residents can still remember milestones on the roads, indicating distance to various towns.
64. (*opposite, below*) Cranleigh High Street today.
65. (*above*) The old Barn, taken from a watercolour of 1883. It stood outside the garden wall of Ivy Hall Farm (now Lloyds Bank) and a piggery, calf shed, cow stalls and stables were attached. Village boys sailed their rafts on the duck pond which has now been filled in. The War Memorial was built on the site.
66. (*below*) The demolition of the old barn. On the green, either side of the Barn, the Benefit Society held their fair every June. 'Stalls were laid out from the Onslow to the Barn selling ginger breads, cakes, vases, penny toys, china dogs and dolls. The other side of the building was reserved for steam roundabouts, shooting galleries, fortune tellers, peepshows and all kinds of whelk stalls.' In the evening everyone danced on the cricket green to the village band.

67. The barn was demolished in 1887. Although it is always referred to in the village as the 'Old Barn', its correct name was Birdfield Barn. Part of it stood on the site of the present drinking fountain. In the early half of this century, Mr. Beadle the blacksmith used to ride from his smithy opposite the common to the centre of the village and back on his penny-farthing bicycle.

68. Cranleigh women hoeing turnip-tops on A. B. Johnson's farm at New Park during the First World War.

69. Until the latter half of the last century, Cranleigh's working population has mainly been employed on the land. The clay ground was not very productive until in the 1620s Richard Mower of Mannings Hill Farm discovered that lime considerably improved its fertility. This picture shows a haymaking team in the early 1920s at Whipley Farm. The last bullock cart in this vicinity was found in the rickyard and is now in the Weald and Downland Open Air Museum at Singleton.

70. Judging horses at a local show about 1905. Since 1947 Cranleigh has enjoyed an annual agriculture show, until recently held at Knowle Park.

71. Mr. N. Stedman and Harry Frances spreading muck in 1913 on the glebelands, a site now occupied by Cranleigh Comprehensive School. Most of the right hand background of the picture is still open ground belonging to Cranleigh School playing fields. These gentlemen would have been very surprised if they had known that hundreds of children were eventually to be educated on this very spot.

72. It was believed that the Reverend Thurlow managed to have a railway station built at Baynards in exchange for cheap land to the railway company. On 2nd October 1865 a booth was erected behind the station, and a band played on the platform to welcome the first train. Breakfast was provided for 200 guests at Baynards House, in celebration.

73. When the railway was opened a special train was run, decorated with flags and evergreens. A band played and everyone was allowed a free ride. Some indulged in more than one and spent the day riding to Baynards and back.

74. Drawing of the 'Cranleigh Flyer' by Mr. I. B. F. Wyness. Although the locomotive was displayed at Cranleigh station in the 1930s, she never worked the Guildford-Horsham line, being a main-line express.

75. This engine was built sometime after 1884 and ran on the Guildford to Horsham line from 1886 to 1900.

76. 'I never saw the sea until I was 14 years old and then it was to go to Littlehampton–it's a shame the railway has gone because you could go from Cranleigh to Brighton for 2s 6d return. The great excitement of the year was the village outing when the whole village was empty that day. All the women and children went.'

77. Cranleigh School cricketers on the green. At the end of the last century they shared the cricket ground with the villagers and helped with expenses. The ground was first enclosed by Dr. Albert A. Napper in 1856, then treasurer of the club. The pitch consisted of only one acre, and chains had to be removed on match days.

78. Cranleigh School opened within two months of the arrival of the railway in 1865, and was intended for the sons of farmers. Dr. Merriman was the first headmaster, and his pupils consisted of 22 boarders and four day boys. The numbers of boys rapidly increased and buildings were added over the years, until today pupils total 724 boys and girls.

79. (*above*) Cranleigh School boys, photographed in 1879. Pupils reached the school from the railway station by horse cab. The classrooms were described as 'light and airy' in advertisements of the time, but would not give that impression by today's standards. In keeping with school customs of the times, canings were administered as punishment for misdemeanors.

80. (*overleaf*) Cranleigh School pupils taken in 1883. The only playing field at this time was in front of the school. Football, rather than rugger, was played. Dr. Merriman, nicknamed 'Old Joe' by the boys, retired after 27 years' service. Fees were then £30 per annum.

81. Cranleigh School kitchens: in the early years all bread and cakes were baked on the premises, and whole sides of beef and pork were chopped in the kitchen. The stone-flagged floors were scrubbed by hand every day.

82. An early dormitory at Cranleigh School with suitable texts on the wall! The bowls and toothmugs are for early morning ablutions.

83. (*overleaf top*) Cranleigh School sanatorium, which treated minor illnesses, many of them caused by the poor water supply from the school well.

84. (*overleaf below*) The old school tuckshop has now been turned into staff living quarters, and there is a new shop in the main building.

85. (*above*) A very early photograph of the village hospital before any extensions were added.

86. (*below*) Cranleigh had the first cottage hospital in England where the poor could be treated and only pay according to their means. Villagers were very proud of this centre of healing, mostly paid for out of their contributions and fund raising.

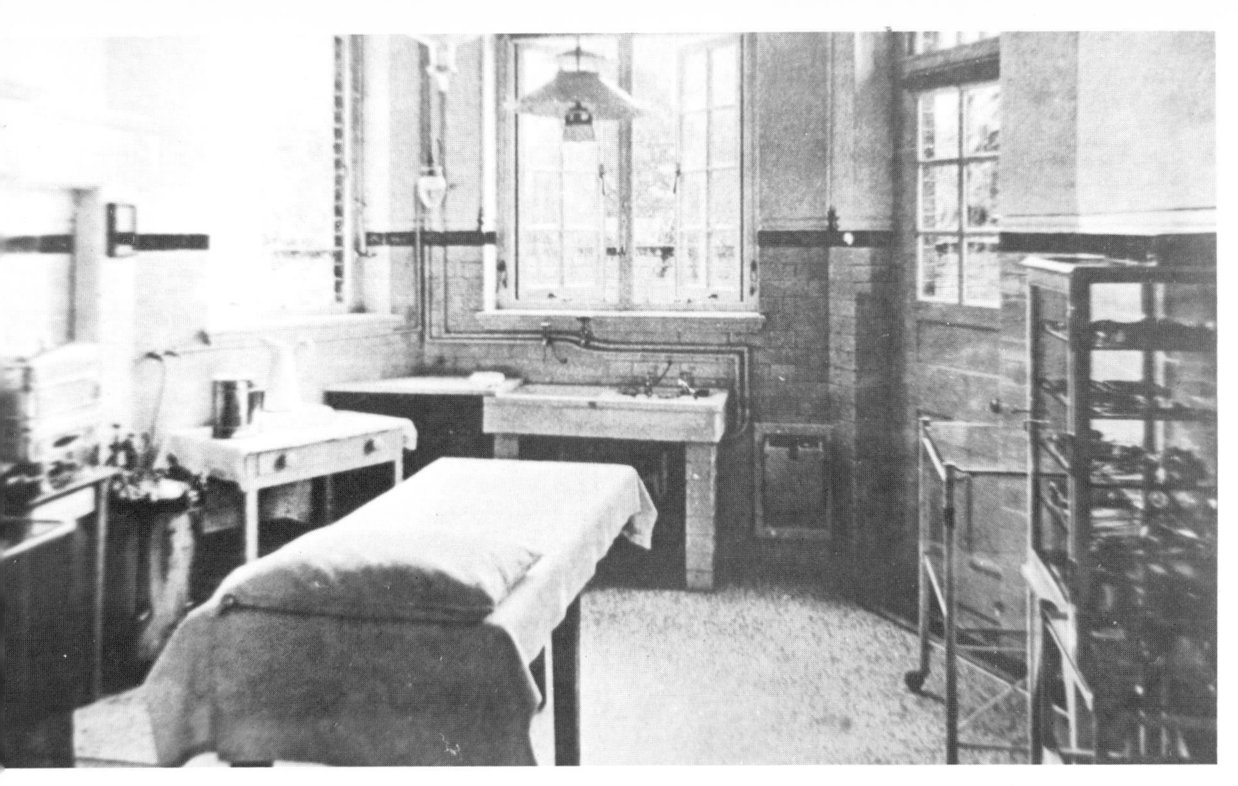

87. (*above*) The hospital operating room, the scene of many amputations and other operations.

88. (*below*) One of the two original hospital wards. Patients paid between 3s. 6d. and 7s. towards their expenses according to their means.

89. Dr. Arthur was succeeded by his son, Dr. Albert A. Napper, in 1867, who practised locally for 54 years. He was described as a fine handsome man who rode on horseback to his patients in all weathers.

+ CRANLEIGH AMBULANCE CORPS +

90. (*overleaf, above*) Cranleigh Emergency Team, probably after 1913. The wheels were added to the stretcher in 1910, reducing the risk of jarring the patients.
From left to right: J. Charman, W. Kitcher, H. Wright, P. Bixley, J. Boyd and G. Hook.

91. (*overleaf, below*) Dr. Walker, a local Cranleigh practitioner, was responsible for forming the Ambulance Corps in Cranleigh in 1896, which in 1900 became the Cranleigh Ambulance Corps. It was disbanded in 1913.

92. (*above*) Ambulance transport had greatly improved by 1928!

93. Mrs. Joan Bradshaw of Knowle gave the drinking fountain to Cranleigh in 1889 in memory of her third son, as well as the church lychgate in memory of her husband.

94. The old Village Hall, now the British Legion building. The modern village hall is in the village centre.

CRANLEIGH AMBULANCE

95. (*opposite above*) This new fire engine was too large to be housed under the village hall so was kept at the ambulance station. Back row, left to right: George Batchelor (driver), Jack Barnfield, Teddy Dicker, Ted Sandford, George Tanner; front row: Jim Sandford, Tom Sandford, Jack Butcher, Cecil Watkinson and Ted Budgen.

96. (*opposite below*) Cranleigh fire engine decorated for the village show.

97. (*above*) The old manual fire engine.

98. (*below*) These old tenements became almshouses for the homeless in 1821, and were demolished in 1885 when the Lady Peak institute was built there as a memorial to her. The institute now serves as a library and citizens' advice bureau.

99. (*below*) Ivy Hall Farm, which is now known as Tyler's grocery shop. This old farmhouse became a post office at the beginning of the century. The ivy-covered wall supported by huge buttresses ran from the farmhouse to Carol House, enclosing the farm garden.

100. (*opposite above*) Mr. and Mrs. E. L. Rowcliffe lived at Hall Place estate which incorporated Barrihurst Farm, High Billingshurst and Home Farms. Mr. Rowcliffe was not only responsible for the maple trees on the Common but also the fountain outside Barrihurst. This house was occupied by Canadians during the Second World War and fell into disrepair. It was sold in 1949 and used by the Council to shelter temporarily homeless families. It has now been pulled down and a number of new houses built on the grounds.

101. (*opposite below*) A group of maidservants on their 'day off' playing a game of cards. They were employed by Mrs. Rowcliffe of Hall Place. Mary Fuller sits on the far right and Rose Ford is behind her. Old villagers can still remember Mrs. Rowcliffe driving through Cranleigh in her carriage 'looking very regal'. The Rowcliffes were noted for their lavish shooting parties.

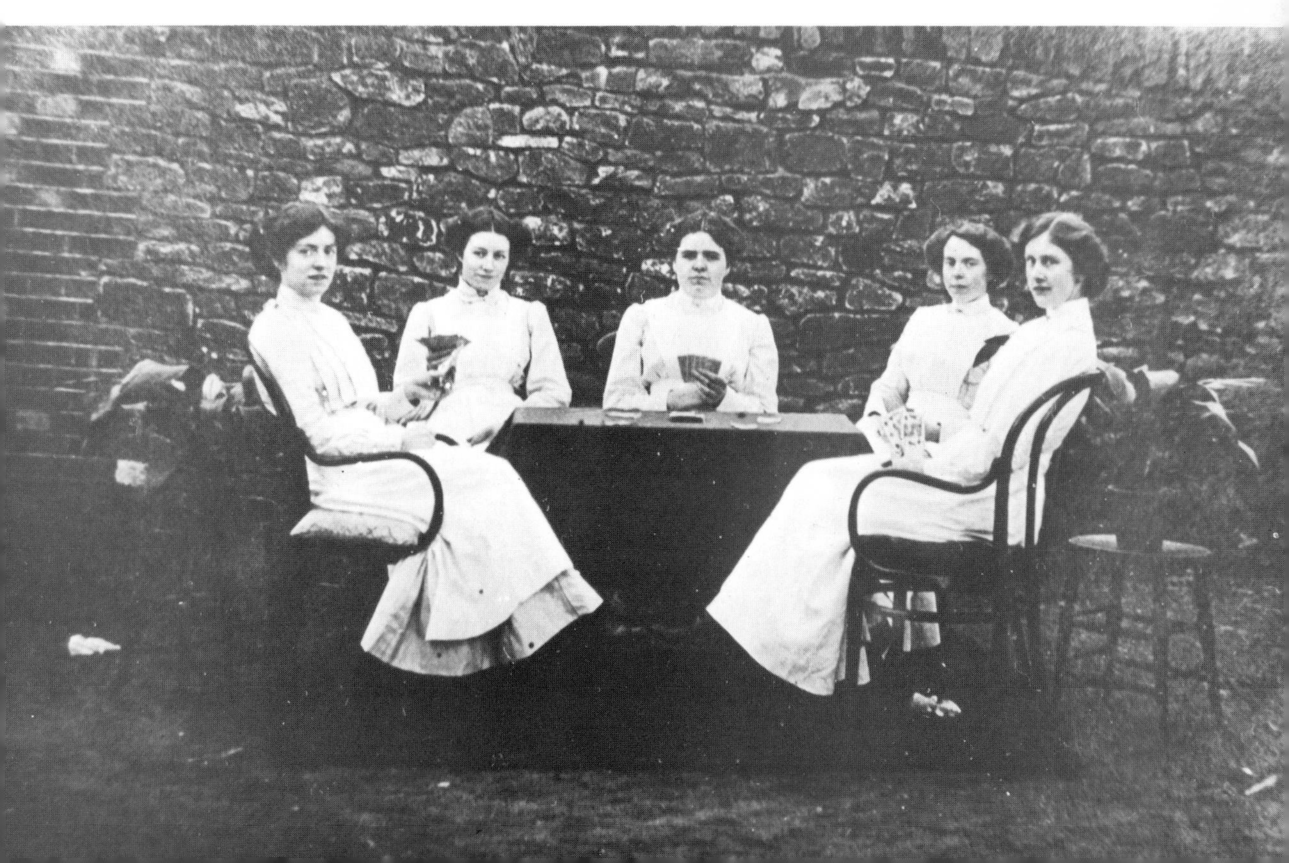

102. Baynards Manor was described as 'a fair noble residence with an avenue of trees up to it'. It was built of mellow red bricks, with a roof covered in Horsham slabs. Some of the original walls were three feet thick. The windows of the chief rooms were of fine painted glass.

103. Richard Budgen lived at Hall Place and was employed by the Rowcliffes and also worked at nearby Hawkins Farm. A neighbouring farmer can remember when as a small boy he would often visit Mr. Budgen to inspect a stuffed deformed two-headed calf which hung on the cottage wall. When Mr. Budgen died, the neighbour acquired the heads and has put them in his private farm museum.

104. The original Knowle House was built in the year 1303 by Robert of Knoll or Knole and contained 'a large banqueting hall, two butteries and a spacious parlour in the western wing'. The house fell into decay and was rebuilt in 1823 by Walter Hanham using some of the oak panelling from the old building. The Onslow family still bear the name associated with our parish.

105. The lodge-keeper's house in Knowle Lane, 1920.

106. (*opposite above*) A photograph of Knowle Lane taken around the turn of the century.

107. (*opposite below*) The two lodges of Knowle House at the entrance to Knowle Lane. The one on the right hand side became Cranleigh post office for many years, but is now a restaurant and shop. The lodge on the left became part of the old Co-operative shop which has recently been demolished and the ground awaits further development.

108. (*above*) This picture shows part of the cottage, named Cromwell Cottage, where Cromwell's men were stationed when he stayed at Knowle in 1657.

109. (*above*) Eli Hampshire, photographed in his shepherd's smock, lived in the village of Ewhurst from 1834-1896. He became very concerned over the plight of the poor in Cranleigh and Ewhurst, and after teaching himself to read and write from his family Bible, wrote to the Prime Minister, Mr. Gladstone, suggesting improvements to the Poor Law. He also wrote two books about the poverty around him.

110. Mr. Randall, a bootmaker, and his family lived in a house which stood on the site of the present Barclay's Bank in Cranleigh High Street. On the right hand side of the photograph can be seen the roof of the *Greyhound* public house, long since pulled down. An annual fair was held in the field behind the pub, and on Saturdays a stall sold whelks in front of the building.

111. (*opposite*) Stephen Rowland was a great local benefactor. He founded the local Gas Company in 1876 and became its chairman, and brought a public water supply from the springs at Nore Farm, Hascombe in 1886. Later, he developed the New Park estate and surrounding roads and bridges. He lived to be 100 years old.

112. (*right*) This picture, taken in 1857, shows Mr. Henry Rowland's house (uncle to Mr. Stephen Rowland), which stood next to Cranley House. It was once owned by a family called Richbells, thought to be descended from French glassworkers, who settled in the district in the 15th century. Stephen Rowland lived in his uncle's house when he was a boy. It is still standing and has been converted into a wine bar.

113. (*below*) Mr. Windsor's coal cart delivering warmth to his chilly customers. This picture was taken outside the old post office. In earlier days, only the rich could afford the coal which was transported from South Wales by canal and unloaded at Elmbridge wharf.

114. Mrs. Sandford and her mother at the turn of the century. St Andrew's church is in the background, and the old barn at the back of the building has now been turned into a cottage.

115. Apple Tree Cottage overlooks the cricket ground. Many years after this photograph was taken it was used as a tea room, but has now been enlarged and is a private residence.

116. Mr. Stemp, an old Cranleigh villager wearing his smock, and with him Tom Smallpiece.

117. This old painting of High Upfold, an Elizabethan farmhouse, is dated 1889. In 1847 the farm was owned and occupied by yeoman James Elmes and his two sisters. A very old iron fireback, dated 1598, and made at a local iron works, was found in this house. High Upfold is now part of Cranleigh School and has been modernised. The outbuilding and barn have become the VIth form centre and small concert hall for senior pupils.

118. Wyphurst House, taken in 1924, when the estate was split up and sold. This mansion belonged to the Wyphurst Estate; part of the house dates back to the 16th century. It was reconstructed and added to in 1907. Local people were employed in the house and on the estate. The house is now St Joseph's Special School.

119. Rydinghurst House, where Mr. Croxford, the cobbler, worked as a garden boy, and where a head gardener and two under-gardeners were also employed. The boy was responsible for cleaning the boots and shoes, carrying indoors the coal and wood for fires, polishing the knives in a machine (after which they had to be rubbed with an emery board) and weeding the tennis courts.

120. Looking across from the flooded Lucks Green on the Horsham Road towards the High Street. Due to the storm water pouring down from the hills, Cranleigh has endured many floods over the years, but the drainage system has now been modernised and drains wide enough to contain the excess water have been installed.

121. This wedding was held at the bride's home, called Little Park Hatch Cottage, when Miss Hilda Parsons married a Mr. Worsfold in the early 1900s. This cottage has now become *Little Park Hatch* public house. The little girl on the right was Lilly Parsons, aged 2½ years. She is now Mrs. Wooten, aged 73 and living near Portsmouth.

122. A view from Lucks Green looking up the flooded Horsham Road. The thick black mud covered the cottagers' gardens, ruining the produce so carefully cultivated for the local horticultural show. Water even seeped into the strong room of the local London and County Bank, flooding it to a depth of five feet.

123. Floods outside Oliver House and Cromwell Cottage in 1903.

124. During a tremendous thunderstorm in 1903 torrential rain poured down from the surrounding hills. Alarmed villagers left their beds and assembled in the streets. The worst areas of devastation were the Ewhurst Road, Horsham Road and Cranleigh High Street, where the water reached a depth of two feet, and Knowle Lane, where mounds of gravel and stones blocked the railway crossing and stopped the trains.

125. Parkhouse Cottages, on the Common. Photographed in 1918 and showing the cricket green in the left background. Animals are no longer allowed to graze on the common, and it has been taken over for cricket and football. The village fairs are now held on the part shown in the foreground. The cottages were thought to have been built for railway workers. The Cranleigh Workhouse was situated behind the house on the right-hand corner.

126. Mr. and Mrs. Pirie and the bakery delivery van about to set out on the rounds. This cottage and the bakery have now been converted into a private house and the garden has become one of the attractions for Cranleigh visitors.

127. Mr. and Mrs. Pirie made and sold their own baked bread at this charming shop on Cranleigh Common, using flour from the windmill which stood opposite their premises. When Archdeacon Sapte attended the opening ceremony of St Andrew's church next door, they supplied the hot supper which followed the event.

128. The St Andrew's bakery cart setting off to deliver bread and groceries. Mr. Pirie and his twin sons are standing in front of their 17th-century home, once called St Andrew's Cottage and which is now a listed building.

129. St Andrew's church, on the Common, was built to ease the overcrowding in the parish church. The foundation stone was laid in 1897 by Archdeacon Sapte. It has now been demolished and replaced by flats for the elderly.

130. This house on Smithwood Common, known as Maplewood Farm House, is now divided into two cottages. In 1846 it was occupied by a Mr. John Whitbourne. At that time the common was a lonely place crossed by cart tracks and paths. On the other side of the common was the *Peewit* beer house kept by Meshach May, which is now the *Four Elms* public house.

131. Smithwood Farm House, from a water colour painted in 1883. The house was built in the 15th century and additions and alterations were made at a later date. The chimney was not built until the 17th century. In earlier days the smoke used to pass through a hole in the roof. Traces of soot in the rafters of the crown post roof are evidence of these early times.

132. In the First World War the Oaklands Red Cross Auxiliary Hospital was run by Mrs. E. L. Rowcliffe of Hall Place estate. This photograph, taken from the Joint War Committee Report, 1914-1919, shows the staff in 1918.

133. A 'fol-de-rols' concert party to entertain the troops at Oaklands Hospital in 1917.

134. Red Cross nurses and wounded soldiers at Oaklands, Knowle Lane. This old house has now been pulled down and a new dwelling erected on the site.

135. The 5th battalion of the Oxfordshire and Buckinghamshire Light Infantry were stationed in tents on the Common near the banks for a short period. Here they are shown lined up for inspection.

136. The soldiers of the Oxfordshire and Buckinghamshire Light Infantry marching through Cranleigh High Street after church parade, Christmas 1914.

137. A First World War parade on the cricket green, Cranleigh. The 1914-18 war brought tragedy to the small rural village. Many of its young men were killed. Mr. Henly, the late village policeman remembered some of his friends—two brothers killed within a fortnight of one another, two of the postman's sons killed one after the other, and another boy killed within three weeks of arriving in France.

138. Cranleigh cricket ground now consists of seven acres of beautiful turf, said to be second only in England to Oval. Most famous players have batted on this turf, including the Bedser twins, Peter May, Jack Hobbs, Ted Dexter Keith Miller, Leary Constantine and E. W. S. Swanton (a Cranleighan).

139. Cranleigh cricket team. In the back row the three men on the right were Eric Kilick, Frank Gardener and Dobbin Mann. In the front row were, at the left hand side, Frank Warren and on the right, George Gill. The photograph was taken in front of the old thatched pavilion. The cricket ground used to be mowed with a mower drawn by a horse which wore leather shoes to avoid damaging the pitch.

140. (*above*) In 1843 the cricket ground was mainly used for grazing cattle, but by 1845 Dr. Napper, the Squire, and five members of the Street family organised regular cricket games. At one time a complete team was composed entirely of Streets. After the Second World War the thatch of this well-loved wooden cricket pavilion caught fire and was destroyed. It was later replaced by a new brick building worthy of its picturesque setting.

141. (*below*) A Punch and Judy show given by Mr. Burgess, the local jeweller, at the village flower show.

142. (*overleaf*) Cranleigh and District British Legion Tug-of-War Team. From left to right: W. H. Brown, P. Bartlett, C. R. Beadell, C. A. V. Hook, E. Buckman, A. Jarrard, C. Buckman. Bottom row: D. Buckman, R. Buckman, G. V. Hayman, G. Thoday, and the coach and trainer, G. Buckman and S. Buckman.

143. (*overleaf*) Cranleigh football team came into being in 1891. In 1906 the team names were: standing— E. Farnfield, R. B. Caws, P. Stanton, Dr. Napper, W. Stevens, J. Elliott, W. Farnfield, J. Clayton: and sitting— E. Boxall, H. Buckman, J. A. Steeds, E. Stevens, L. Stewardson.

144. (*above*) Two packs of foxhounds regularly hunted in the Cranleigh area, the Chiddingfold Hunt (whose kennels were stationed at Dunsfold) and the Surrey Union Hunt (headquarters at Oakwood Hill). The Guildford and Shere beagles also met in this vicinity. This picture was taken at a 'meet' outside the *Three Horseshoes* public house.

145. (*below*) Cranleigh tennis tournament, 1923. The first tournament was held in 1922 and, as an incentive, a cup was presented to the men in 1923. The first ladies' singles cup was awarded in 1924. With the exception of the war years, the tournament was held annually on Cranleigh cricket common.

146. This old yew tree was clipped by Matthew Taylor in 1850 to resemble the cock on the church tower.

147. The Cranleigh band, affectionately called the 'Spit and Dribble', leading this procession in the Ewhurst Road. They are passing the old village hall, now out of sight on the right.

148. Cranleigh brass band in about 1904. In the back row, 7th from the left, is George Sandford; 8th from the left is Jim Sandford. In the middle row 5th from left, Harry Sandford.

149. Cranleigh brass and reed band on the occasion of the Southern Counties Challenge Cup competition in 1913. Front row; H. Ketcher, 2nd from left, E. W. Fuller, extreme right; second row: C. Stephens, 2nd from left, G. Ansell, extreme right; back row: H. Lee, extreme left, J. Sandford, next to Mr. Lee, C. Charman, 4th from right.

150. A humorous postcard.

151. A humorous postcard.

Windlesham
Woodham lane
Hill
Chertsey
Horsyl
Bagshot
Wisley
Esher
EMLEY
Cobham
Bysley
Bitlöor
Cobham Street
Bagshot
HVNDRED
Pursford
Cobham
Frimley
Woking
Stoke Dabernon
Breakwood
Newark
Ockam
Slyfeyld
WOKING
Ripley
HVN:
Fetcham
Great Bokham
Purbright
Bradley
Seude
Preston
Effingham
Mayfort
Henley Park
Sutton
DRED
Little Bokham
East Horsley
Robarns
Polsdon
Worplesdon
Burphants
West Horsley
Westwoode
Stowghton
East Clandon
Aslie
Stoke
Wotton
Wanboro
Gulford manor
West Clandon
Meroc
Wyke
Guildford
BLACKHEATH
Katorm hill
Poyk
Puttenham
Littleton
Tilling
Abinger
Shore
Gumshall
Lothes: ley
Set Martins
Sweland
Polsted
Shalford
Chilworth
Ham
Compton
Albury
Fernecombe
Tongly
Weston
NDRE
Estsil
Shackleford
Holmbury
Nusted
Ognersh
Peperhare
BLACKHEATH
Bramley
Godalming
Catteshill
THE REGNI
Esing
Milford
OR WOTTON
Mounsted
Oxmforde
Wheterstrete
Ewhurst
Burgate
Hascomb
Scotsland
Cranley
GODALMING
Enton
HVNDRED
Hameldon
Knole
Thursley
Farncombe
Vachery
Witley
Nore
Whitley park
HVNDRED
Baynards
Lexley
Embhome
Dunsfold
Grashouse
Awfold
Pophole
Shotouer mill
Chidingfold
Sydey
Warningfold
Rydgwick
SHIRE